PERTH
HISTORY TOUR

First published 2020

Amberley Publishing
The Hill, Stroud,
Gloucestershire, GL5 4EP
www.amberley-books.com

Copyright © Jack Gillon, 2020
Map contains Ordnance Survey data
© Crown copyright and database
right [2020]

The right of Jack Gillon to be
identified as the Author of this work
has been asserted in accordance with
the Copyrights, Designs and Patents
Act 1988.

British Library Cataloguing in
Publication Data.
A catalogue record for this book is
available from the British Library.

ISBN 978 1 3981 0141 8 (print)
ISBN 978 1 3981 0142 5 (ebook)

Origination by Amberley Publishing.
Printed in Great Britain.

INTRODUCTION

One would have thought that there was no Perth man (out of the asylum) who would not have rejoiced in his unstained tranquillity, in the delightful heights that enclose him – in his silvery Tay – in the quiet beauty of his green and level Inches.

Lord Cockburn, *Journals*, 1874

There is some debate about the origin of the name Perth. It is said to derive either from a Pictish word for wood or copse or from *Aber-tha*, meaning the mouth of the Tay. For centuries Perth was known as St John's Toun (or St Johnstoun), from its association with its church dedicated to John the Baptist.

The location of Perth, at the lowest crossing point of the Tay, was fundamental to its development and it has been inhabited since prehistoric times. Its location close to Scone, with its royal connections, was an important factor in the growth of the settlement. It was the effective capital of Scotland until the mid-fifteenth century and an important religious centre.

Perth was given Royal Burgh status in the early twelfth century under King David I and developed as one of the most affluent towns in Scotland. The navigable River Tay was a significant factor in the prosperity of the town: ships could sail up the river and the harbour carried out an extensive foreign trade. Perth also had a thriving industrial base in leather, linen and metalwork.

Perth, however, suffered its fair share of troubles from invading armies, outbreaks of the plague and destructive floods.

In the nineteenth century, whisky production, insurance and dyeing were additions to Perth's traditional industries and burgeoning economy. The first railway station in Perth opened in 1848, further enabling expansion, and the city became known as the 'Gateway to the Highlands'.

An outward sign of this growing prosperity was the 'improvement schemes of considerable magnitude which were adopted and carried out' – new grid-plan developments of elegant Georgian terraces to the north and south sides of the town were built and the old medieval layout of the town was rationalised.

Perth has been known for centuries as the *Fair City*. However, in the late 1990s the government decided that it no longer met the criteria for city status. This was rectified on 14 March 2012, when Perth was reinstated as an official city, as part of the Queen's Diamond Jubilee celebrations.

Perth is central to Scotland and its history, and today it is a charming historic city that retains much of its ancient character and architectural quality. Modern-day Perth is a thriving city; its retail centre has an attractive pedestrianised high street and a wide variety of shops, cafés, museums, galleries, restaurants and pubs.

The tour starts at St John Street and follows a route around the centre of the town. The final item is Kinnoull Tower, which is more out of the town. The bracing trek up Kinnoull Hill to view the Tower is rewarded by magnificent views over the River Tay and beyond from the steep south-facing summit.

KEY

1. Church of St John the Baptist
2. St John Street
3. Perth Mercat Cross
4. St John's Square
5. Perth City Hall, King Edward Street
6. South Street
7. The Salutation Hotel, Nos 30–36 South Street
8. The Victoria Bridge
9. Queen's Bridge
10. Tay Street
11. Post Office/General Accident, Tay Street/High Street
12. Perth from Barnhill
13. Marshall Place
14. Marshall Place Floods
15. Princes Street
16. St Leonard's-in-the Fields Free Church, Marshall Place
17. Entrance to South Inch at Marshall Place
18. Boating Pond, South Inch
19. Perth Railway Station
20. Infirmary/Library, York Place
21. Waverley Hotel, York Place
22. Kinnoull Street
23. The Former Sandeman Library, Kinnoull Street
24. J. Pullar & Sons of Perth
25. High Street
26. High Street, The Fair Maid
27. George Street
28. View from the Royal George Hotel
29. George Hotel, Queen Victoria
30 and 31. Perth Bridge
32. End of the Old Bridge
33. Bridgend Main Street
34. North Inch
35. North Inch Bandstand
36. Sport on the North Inch
37. The Boat Station, North Inch
38. North Inch, The Lynedoch Monument
39. Prince Albert Memorial, Charlotte Street
40. Charlotte Street
41. Rose Terrace
42. Atholl Street
43. St Ninian's Cathedral, Atholl Street and North Methven Street
44. Fair Maid's House, North Port Street (Curfew Row)
45. Balhousie Castle, Hay Street
46. Kinnoull Tower

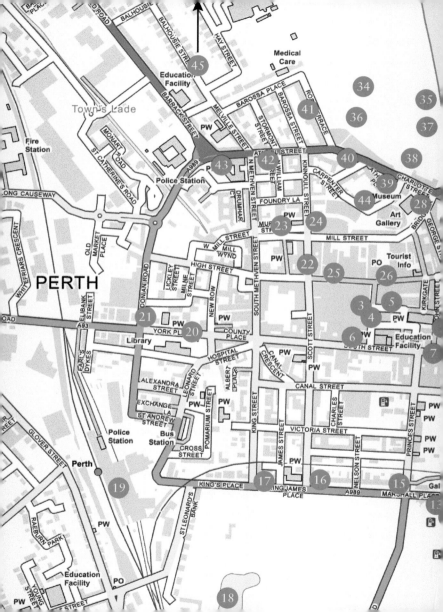

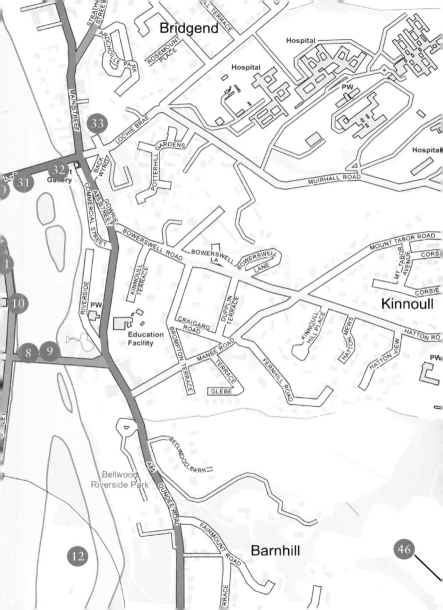

1. CHURCH OF ST JOHN THE BAPTIST

The Church of St John the Baptist is Perth's oldest surviving building. The original church was completed by 1241, although most of the present structure dates from between 1440 and 1500. The church was central to life in the town, which was known as St John's Toun (or St Johnstoun). In 1923, the church was extensively renovated and restored by Sir Robert Lorimer as a memorial to the people of Perth who lost their lives in the First World War.

2. ST JOHN STREET

St John Street was developed in the early nineteenth century on the line of the old Ritten Row to improve access to the new bridge. It is lined by elegant terraces with ground-floor shops.

4. ST JOHN'S SQUARE

Above: The St John's Square's mixed-use development of housing, shops and offices was the result of redevelopment in the 1960s. It was relatively short-lived and was itself redeveloped as the Saint John's Centre in the 1990s. The mercat cross has endured through all the changes in this area.

3. PERTH MERCAT CROSS

Opposite: Perth's early mercat cross stood on the High Street opposite Skinnergate – the site is marked by an octagon of stones. In 1651, the cross was pulled down by Cromwell to supply stones for his Citadel on the South Inch. Another cross was erected in 1669, but it proved an obstruction to traffic and was removed in 1765. The present cross in St John's Square was erected in 1913 as a memorial to Edward VII.

5. PERTH CITY HALL, KING EDWARD STREET

King Edward Street was completed in 1902 as a new street linking the High Street and South Street. The new City Hall was opened on 29 April 1911. Its imposing baroque frontage dominates the east side of the street. The hall has been disused since Perth's new concert hall opened in 2005.

D VII MEMORIAL AND CITY HALL. PERTH.

6. SOUTH STREET

South Street was once the site of Perth's weekly shoe market and was known as the Shoe Gait. It was originally terminated at its east end by Gowrie House. Direct access to the river was made on the demolition of the house in the early nineteenth century and South Street became a busy through route when the Victoria Bridge was opened in 1900.

7. THE SALUTATION HOTEL, NOS 30–36 SOUTH STREET

The Salutation Hotel lays claim to being the longest-established hotel in Scotland. It was a coaching inn between 1699 and 1745, and was the main resting point on the coach roads from Edinburgh and Glasgow to Aberdeen and Inverness. The name, the Salutation, is said to derive from John Burt, an early landlord, having shaken hands with Prince Charlie, who stayed at the hotel in 1745.

8. THE VICTORIA BRIDGE

As road traffic built up at the end of the nineteenth century, it was clear that a second crossing of the Tay was required to relieve pressure on the Old Bridge. The Victoria Bridge was opened by Lady Pullar in 1900. It was a steel truss bridge spanning between concrete piers.

9. QUEEN'S BRIDGE

The Queen's Bridge was opened by the Queen on 10 October 1960, as a replacement for the Victoria Bridge. The date was significant as the 750th anniversary of the granting of the royal charter of 1210 to Perth. It is a light and graceful structure of shallow arches. The old bridge was ingeniously jacked-up and the new pre-stressed concrete bridge slotted in beneath it to allow traffic to keep crossing the Tay.

10. TAY STREET

The Watergate was old Perth's most impressive street, lined by fine houses with long narrow garden plots stretching down to the Tay. It rapidly lost its status when Tay Street, the new grand boulevard along the bank of the river, was opened in the mid-1870s. The clutter of medieval backlands was removed and the city presented an imposing new frontage to the river.

11. POST OFFICE/GENERAL ACCIDENT, TAY STREET/HIGH STREET

Perth's elegant-looking old post office at the east end of the High Street was opened in 1860 and removed in 1898 for the redevelopment of the site as the General Accident headquarters.

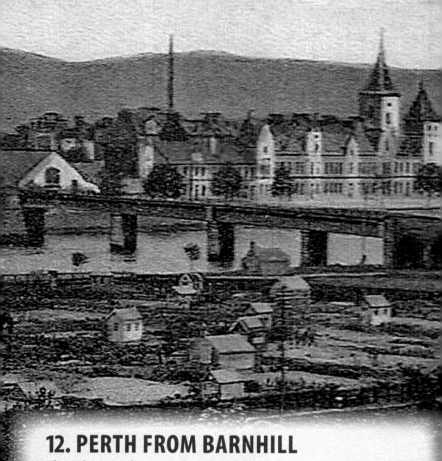

12. PERTH FROM BARNHILL

The rail service from Dundee to Perth began in 1827, but terminated at Barnhill on the east side of the river until a wooden railway bridge across the Tay was opened in 1849. The new railway bridge, which openend in 1862, was one of the first large plate-girder bridges in Scotland.

13. MARSHALL PLACE

Marshall Place was built from 1806 and was intended to be the first part of a grand scheme to create a Southern New Town of Georgian terraces. Marshall Place takes its name form Provost Thomas Hay Marshall. Marshall (1768–1808) was a Baillie at age twenty-two and twice provost. Marshall was the inspiration behind many improvements in Perth, including the development of numerous new streets of elegant Georgian architecture.

14. MARSHALL PLACE FLOODS

The fast-flowing waters of the Tay have been the source of a number of extreme floods. The first recorded was in 1210. In 1621, Perth Bridge was destroyed and the highest flood level ever recorded was in 1814. The image of a flooded Marshall Place is from August 1910. Flood defence works with embankments, walls, floodgates and pumping stations, completed in 2001 at a cost £25million, now protect the city.

Pri

15. PRINCES STREET

Princes Street was developed in the late eighteenth century to link the Edinburgh Road with the new bridge. Princes Street railway station opened on 24 May 1847 on the Perth–Dundee main line. It closed to regular passenger traffic on 28 February 1966. The railway line passes behind Marshall Place and is carried over cross streets by a series of bridges.

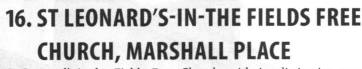

16. ST LEONARD'S-IN-THE FIELDS FREE CHURCH, MARSHALL PLACE

St Leonard's-in-the Fields Free Church, with its distinctive crown spire, dates from 1885 and forms an impressive landmark on Marshall Place, overlooking the South Inch. It was built as St Leonard's Free Church and designed by the London-based architect John James Stevenson (1831–1908).

17. ENTRANCE TO SOUTH INCH AT MARSHALL PLACE

The South Inch was used as an archery ground, a bleach field, for cattle grazing, horse racing and a burial ground for plague victims. The golf course on the South Inch was popular during the eighteenth century, but was abandoned in 1833, when the Royal Perth Golfing Society moved to the North Inch.

18. BOATING POND, SOUTH INCH

In the 1840s, there were proposals to build a railway station on the South Inch, which provoked outrage amongst the people of Perth and resulted in a petition being submitted to parliament against the loss of their cherished green space. The boating pond at the South Inch was recently given a makeover as part of a project to upgrade facilities at the park.

BOATING POND, SOUTH INCH, PERT

B

19. PERTH RAILWAY STATION

Perth railway station was opened in 1848 by the Scottish Central railway. The station was extended in 1866 and largely reconstructed in 1886. John Menzies opened one of its first bookstalls at Perth station in May 1857. Perth railway station developed as a main hub on the Scottish rail service.

20. INFIRMARY/LIBRARY, YORK PLACE

The building was designed by William Macdonald Mackenzie (1797–1856), Perth's City Architect for thirty years, and opened as the County and City Infirmary in 1837. It was the main hospital for the district, until the Perth Royal opened in 1914. During the First World War it was a Red Cross Hospital, tending for war wounded. It was then used as council offices until it was converted into the AK Bell Library in 1994.

21. WAVERLEY HOTEL, YORK PLACE

The Waverley Hotel was established in around 1900 and was a popular Perth hostelry. When the building closed as a hotel, it was used as a hostel, which also closed in August 2011. The building was badly damaged by a major fire on 17 November 2015.

22. KINNOULL STREET

Kinnoull Street was laid out in 1823. The former Sandeman Library is on the left side of the street and the enormous Pullar's North British Dyeworks in the right background. The Congregational Church is to the right of the former Sandeman Library.

Kinnoull Street, Perth.

23. THE FORMER SANDEMAN LIBRARY, KINNOULL STREET

Locally born benefactor Professor Archibald Sandeman of Queen's College, Cambridge, bequeathed £30,000 to establish a free public library in Perth. The opening ceremony of the library, in October 1898, was performed by the Earl of Roseberry. The Sandeman Library closed in 1994 when the AK Bell Library opened. The building is now occupied by The Sandeman public house.

24. J. PULLAR & SONS OF PERTH

In the late nineteenth century Pullars was the largest dye works in Scotland, employing over 2,600 workers. Pullars was the first company to provide a dry-cleaning service in Britain and pioneered the use of synthetic dyes. The company operated the largest dry-cleaning machine in the world, capable of cleaning carpets measuring 100 yards square. The building was converted for office use in 2000.

25. HIGH STREET

Perth developed on a plan of two parallel streets, the High Street and South Street, linked by a warren of lanes or vennels leading north and south. The names of these vennels have historic origins and many, such as Cow Vennel and Fleshers Vennel, reflect the trades associated with them in the past.

26. HIGH STREET, THE FAIR MAID

The charming statue of the Fair Maid of Perth sitting reading a book on a bench on the High Street is by Graham Ibbeson and was erected in 1995. It is hard to resist taking the opportunity for a photo sitting beside her.

27. GEORGE STREET

George Street was opened as a planned street in 1771 to provide access
to the new bridge. It is named for George III. The curved line of the
road emphasises the dome of the Perth Museum and Art Gallery,
which can be seen at the far end of the street. The gallery dates from
1824, with an art deco extension of 1931, and commemorates Perth's
Provost Thomas Marshall.

28. VIEW FROM THE ROYAL GEORGE HOTEL

The George Hotel opened in 1773. It originally served as a coaching inn, with stabling for the mail coaches that stopped at Perth's first post office, over the road from the George. It also provided accommodation and refreshment for travellers. The hotel was considerably expanded by its enterprising landlord, William Steele, who took over the premises in the 1900s.

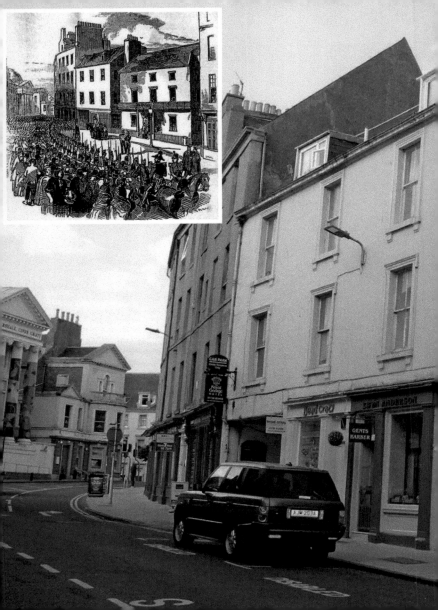

29. GEORGE HOTEL, QUEEN VICTORIA

Queen Victoria arrived for a surprise overnight stay at the George Hotel on 29 September 1848. The hotel was only given a few hours' notice of the arrival of the royal party and had to make hasty arrangements for the visit. The Queen had never stayed in a hotel before and was so impressed by the welcome she received that she granted the hotel a royal Warrant.

30. PERTH BRIDGE

In 1765, an Act of Parliament approved the construction of the bridge. The eminent engineer, John Smeaton (1724–92), who is regarded as the 'father of civil engineering' was appointed to design the bridge, which was completed in October 1771. Smeaton's elegant nine-arch structure in local sandstone was, at 272 metres (893 feet), the longest in Scotland when it opened.

31. PERTH BRIDGE

The bridge was designed to withstand the highest-level spates on the Tay and was tested some three years after it opened when ice blocked the river and parts of the town were flooded. The bridge stood firm and has survived many subsequent floods. The river levels during floods are recorded on the north face of the bridge's pier. The bridge was widened in 1869 to cope with increased traffic.

32. END OF THE OLD BRIDGE

A halfpenny toll was charged to cross the bridge until 1883. A sign on the old toll house specifies the bridge rules: 'No locomotive shall pass upon or over Perth Bridge between the hours of 10am and 3pm and at other times the person in charge of such locomotives shall send a man with a red flag to the opposite end of the bridge from that on which he is to enter, warning all persons concerned of the approach of the locomotive.'

East Bridge Street, Perth

35. NORTH INCH BANDSTAND

The bandstand was located on the west side of the North Inch. It was gifted by James Pullar. The opening concert was a performance by the band of the 6th Royal Dragoons on 25 July 1891. The bandstand was a popular venue during the summer months, with bands providing musical entertainment. In 1959, the bandstand was declared unsafe, demolished and sold for scrap.

36. SPORT ON THE NORTH INCH

The North Inch has always been a popular venue for sporting activities. A racecourse ran around the perimeter until it moved to Scone in 1908. The North Inch was also an important venue for cricket – the first recorded match was in 1849. The North Inch golf course had six holes in 1803, which was increased to eighteen by Old Tom Morris in 1892. The North Inch hosted the Open in 1864 and 1866.

39. PRINCE ALBERT MEMORIAL, CHARLOTTE STREET

The 8-foot-high statue of Prince Albert overlooks Charlotte Street at the southern end of the North Inch. Prince Albert is depicted in the robes of the Order of the Thistle and holding a plan of the Crystal Palace. The memorial was unveiled by Queen Victoria in 1864, three years after Albert's death.

40. CHARLOTTE STREET

Charlotte Street was laid out in 1783 with ordered elegant buildings. The plaque on the wall at the corner of Charlotte Street and Atholl Terrace in the newer image marks the location of the Blackfriars Monastery. It also commemorates the Battle of the North Inch and the murder of King James I at the monastery in 1437.

46. KINNOULL TOWER

The picturesque Kinnoull Tower is a romantic folly on the edge of a dramatic rocky outcrop and forms a major local landmark. It was built by 1829 by Lord Grey of Kinfauns, who had been inspired by castles perched on hills in the Rhine Valley.